PARTNERS

The Grand Prix Horses

ridden by

Ian Millar

Mary-Ellen Dick

Cover: Big Ben, Ian, & Warrior
Photo: Steve Forrester, Perth Courier

ISBN - 13 978-1523996193
ISBN - 10 1523996196

Foreword:

Lynn Millar and I got to know Mary-Ellen and
Kenneth Dick in the early nineteen seventies, over
forty-five years ago. Our relationship has had great
range. We are first and always friends, but there has
been much more. We have been business partners in
horses and real estate. Mary-Ellen worked with us here
at Millar Brooke. Kenneth helped with our vehicle
requirements. And both Mary-Ellen and Kenneth have
been great supporters of Jonathon and Amy in their journey
to the top of the show jumping world. But most important
to me and my family was Mary-Ellen's friendship and support
of Lynn in her time of need.

You will notice in the preface that Mary-Ellen created this book
as a gift for Lily in Lynn's memory, and nothing shows that more
than the dedication page picturing Lynn with "Pokey" and Lily with
"Calvin Klein". The expressions, the body language, the genetics!

When Mary-Ellen contacted me about this book, I was of course intrigued.
I had difficulty listing all of the wonderful Grand Prix horses that I have
competed with over the years. She has done a remarkable job of cataloguing
all of them, most with photographs.

I hope that all who meet or revisit my equine "Partners" through this book will
greatly appreciate them, for I certainly do. They have been the essential ingredient
in my life and career.

Ian Millar
November 22, 2016

Preface:

My thanks to the Millar family for so graciously allowing me
to compile this book. When I came up with the idea, I thought
that it would be a relatively easy task, - simply whip up a little
booklet listing all of Ian's Grand Prix horses with photos and
a short story for each of them.

The reality was that it was a daunting task, - so many horses,
so many years, so many memories! What to include? What
to exclude? Overwhelmed by the body of work, I shelved the
project for several years. That proved to be a good move, for
during that time several new horses were added to the list.

Time passed and then, while out walking on a beautiful winter
day in January 2016, my thoughts turned to the Olympics and
I knew it was time to complete the project. My original concept
of the book was simply to create a record of all the talented equine
athletes that partnered with Ian in the Grand Prix competitions.
By abandoning the idea of including short stories for each horse,
the project became more manageable. The end result (which falls
somewhere between a list and a book) includes the names of the
horses, their owners, and photos where available. My apologies
for any errors or omissions.

I chose the name "Partners" to reflect all of the partnerships that
have worked so well in Ian's life: in business; with horses; with
owners; with friends; with staff; with his children; and most of
all, with his life partner, Lynn.

This book was created as a gift for their granddaughter Lily
in Lynn's memory.

Mary-Ellen Dick

February 14, 2016

For Lynn and Lily

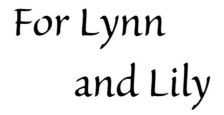

Lily with
Jonathon's GP horse
"Calvin Klein", 2014.

Lynn with her young
homebred colt "Pokey".
Circa 1977/78

<u>Index</u> - chronological listing (approximate) - page 1

<u>Index</u> - chronological listing (approximate) - page 2

Grand Prix Horses

(alphabetically - page 1)

Grand Prix Horses

(alphabetically - page 2)

"The Olympians"

1972 Munich   - Shoeman

1976 Montreal   - Count Down

Alternate Olympics - 1980 Rotterdam   - Brother Sam (Team Gold)

1984 Los Angeles - Big Ben

1988 Seoul   - Big Ben

1992 Barcelona   - Big Ben

1996 Atlanta   - Play It Again

2000 Sydney   - Dorincord

2004 Athens   - Promise Me

2008 Bejing   - In Style (Team Silver)

2012 London   - Star Power

2016 Rio de Janeiro - Dixson qualified, but was sidelined by minor surgery. Ian attended the Olympics as coach for his daughter Amy and her horse Heros.

Ian's very first partner in a Grand Prix (equivalent) class was

"Bayonne Preferred"

Owners: Nancy (Denovan) Woods
and Ian Millar

(no photo available)

"War Machine"

Owner: Doug Cudney

Previous Owners:
Nancy (Denovan) Woods
and Ian Millar

"Beefeater"

Owner: Doug Cudney

(no photo available)

"Shoeman"
Owner: Doug Cudney

Ian Millar schooling Shoeman at Reim, before the Prix de Nations on the Closing Day of the 1972 Olympics

"Blizzard"

Owner: Brigadier-General Denis Whitaker

(no photo available)

Ian at Dwyer Hill Farm

Photo: Debbie Adams

4.

"Night Cat"
Owner: Dwyer Hill Farms

(no photo available)

"Hulio"
Owner: Dwyer Hill Farms

Photo: Debbie Adams

"O'Henry"
Owner: Dwyer Hill Farms

(no photo available)

The early years. Amy & Lynn, Ian & Jonathon (circa 1979)

"Country Club"
Owner: Dwyer Hill Farms

Photo: Bob Foster

photographer: unknown

"Fox Fire"
Owner: Dwyer Hill Farms

Photo:
Debbie Adams

Photo:
Sue Maynard

"Hawk"
Owner: Dwyer Hill Farms

Photo: Debbie Adams

Photo: Debbie Adams

Lynn and Ian in their
improvised rainwear!

(circa 1976-77)

"Bandit"
Owner: Dwyer Hill Farms

Image extracted from a newspaper photo by Ted Shaw

"Springer"
Owner: Dwyer Hill Farms

Photo: Sue Maynard

Photo: Sue Maynard

"Year Of The Cat"
Owner: Dwyer Hill Farms

Photo:
Debbie Adams

Photo: Debbie Adams

"Count Down"
Owner: Dwyer Hill Farms

photographer: unknown

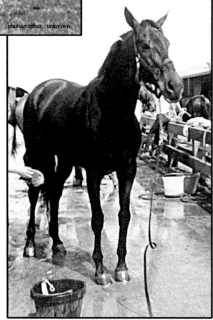

Photographer: unknown

Photo: Debbie Adams

"Brother Sam"

Owner: Dwyer Hill Farms

Subsequent owner: John K. Hoff

"Brother Sam"

Owner: Dwyer Hill Farms

Subsequent owner: John K. Hoff

Photographer unknown

"Magnum"

Owner: Eve Mainwaring

(no photo available)

"Another Brother"

Owner: Dwyer Hill Farms
Subsequent Owners:
Lillian & Fritz Bollinger
and Millar Brooke Farm

Photographer unknown

"Warrior"

Photographer: unknown

Owner: Dwyer Hill Farms
Subsequent owners: Lillian & Fritz Bollinger
and Millar Brooke Farm
Subsequent owner: Canadian Show Jumpers Unltd

17.

"Wotan"

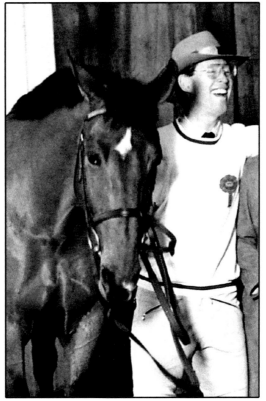

Photographer: unknown

Photo by Judith Buck

Owners: Eve Mainwaring, Roger St. Jacques,
            and Millar Brooke Farm
Subsequent owner: Canadian Show Jumpers Unltd

"Domingo"
Owner: Canadian Show Jumpers Unltd.

Photo: Debbie Adams

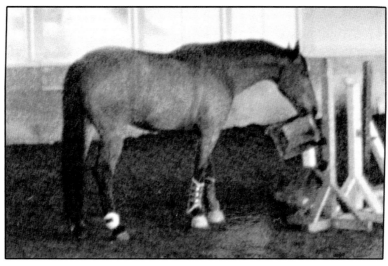

Photo: Debbie Adams

"Isis"

Owner: Ray Lyn Farm

(no photo available)

"Saskia"

Owner: Millar Brooke Farm

(no photo available)

"Foresight"

Owner: Mr. Tom Gayford

Unknown
photographer

"Mission Red"

Owners: Lewis & Lewis/Gymcrack Stables/Millar Brooke Farm

(no photo available)

Some of the Millar Brooke gang, - date unknown

"Extra"
Owner: Juniper Farms

Photo: John Gibson, Calgary Sun

"The Girl Next Door"
Owners: Samantha & Millicent Porteous

(no photo available)

"Czar"
Owner: Vincent Murphy

Photographer: unknown

"Play Back"
Owner: Vincent Murphy

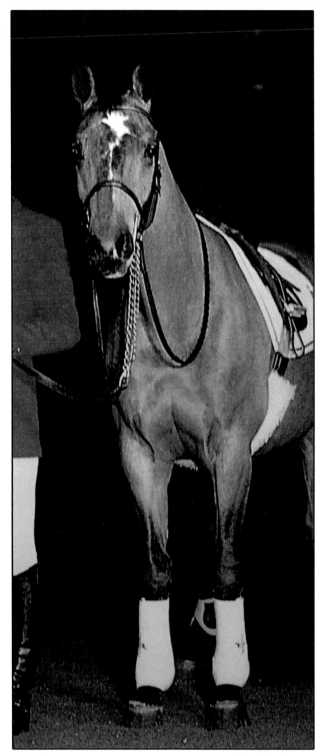

Photographer unknown

"Lucas"
Owner: Lillian & Fritz Bollinger

Photographer: unknown

"Lonely Boy"
Owners: Eve Mainwaring/Jacques Ferland/Millar Brooke Farm

(no photo available)

"Lonesome Dove"
Owners: Lillian & Fritz Bollinger
and Millar Brooke Farm

Photographer unknown

Unknown
photographer

27.

"Winchester"
Owner: Thornbrook Farm

Photo by C. Ross Perry

"Big Ben"

Owners: Eve Mainwaring and Millar Brooke Farm
Subsequent Owner: Canadian Show Jumpers Unltd.

Photo: Cealy Tetley

Photo: Cealy Tetley

Photographer: unknown

29.

"Same Old Song"

Owner: Canadian Show Jumpers Unltd.

(no photo available)

"Baarlo"

Owners: The Baarlo Group

(no photo available)

"My Girl"
Owner: Thornbrook Farm

Unknown
photographer

Photo: Thornbrook Farm

31.

"Canadian Colors"
Owner: Canadian Show Jumpers Unltd.

Photographer: unknown

"Future Vision"
Owner: Horse Futures

Photographer: unknown

"Future Shock"
Owner: Horse Futures

Photographer: unknown

"El Futuro"
Owner: Horse Futures

Photo: Tish Quirk

"Pamino"

Owner: Ray Lyn Farm

(no photo available)

"Ben Again"

Owner: Millar Brooke Farm

Photographer: unknown

36.

"Mistral"

Owner: Millar Brooke Farm
Subsequent Owner: Canadian Show Jumpers Unltd.

Newspaper clipping of photo by Tish Quirk

"Roulette"
Owner: Laura, Jan & Bill Frieder

photographer: unknown

"Emir"
Owner: Millar Brooke Farm

Emir and Jonathon. Photo by M.E. Dick at Millar Brooke Farm

Emir was a Grand Prix partner for both Ian and Jonathon Millar.

"Play It Again"

Owners: Eve Mainwaring, Alan Sandler, and Millar Brooke Farm

Photo: Cealy Tetley

"Future Folly"

Owner: Horse Futures

Photo: Debbie Adams

Ian and Folly at Millar Brooke Farm.
Photo by Lynn Millar

"After Shock"

(El Futuro X Future Shock)

Owners: Bobby Taylor and
            Millar Brooke Farm
Subsequent owners:
            Ann Mathews and
            Millar Brooke Farm

Photo: M.E. Dick

Photo: M.E. Dick

41.

"Life Guard"
Owner: Millar Brooke Farm

Photographer: unknown

Life Guard and Big Ben at home in Millar Brooke arena.

"Ivar"
Owners: Ann Mathews and Millar Brooke Farm

Photo: Cealy Tetley

"Glory Days"
Owner: Millar Brooke Farm

Photo: Cealy Tetley

"Symbari"
Owner: Belle Herbe Farm

Photo: Cealy Tetley

"Pilot's Diamond"
Owners: Ken & Patty Stovel

(no photo available)

"Mont Cenis"
Owners: Ken & Patty Stovel

Photo: Cealy Tetley

"Arnika"
Owner: Henry Williams

Photographer: unknown

"Dorincord"

Owners: Jonathon Millar and the Hendrix family
Subsequent owners: Ann Mathews and
Millar Brooke Farm

Photo: Cealy Tetley

"Promise Me"
Owners: The Baker's Dozen

Photo: Cealy Tetley

"Nicos"
Owner: Todd Snell

Photo: Cealy Tetley

"Jasmine"

Owner: Susan Grange

(no photo available)

"Redefin"
Owner: Susan Grange

"Sweet Dreams"
Owner: Millar Brooke Farm

"Dryden"
Owners: Ariel & Susan Grange

"Stedet's Leroy"
Owner: D K Sporthorses

(no photo available)

"In Style"
Owner: Susan Grange

Photo: Cealy Tetley

Photo: Cealy Tetley

"Star Power"
Owner: Team Works

Photo: Cealy Tetley

Photo: Cealy Tetley

"Dixson"
Owners: Ariel and Susan Grange

Photo: Cealy Tetley

53.

"Baranus"
Owners: The Baranus Group

"Teddy du Bosquetiau"
Owners: Emily and Fiona Kinch

"Vittorio"
Owner: Future Adventures

Photo: Cealy Tetley

Footnote:

In addition to the horses named in this book, there were a few others
which were shown by Ian in Grand Prix classes. However they
weren't listed because he only rode them on one or two occasions.

Manufactured by Amazon.ca
Bolton, ON

33570080R00043